How Many Ways Can You Cut a Pie?

by Jane Belk Moncure
illustrated by Linda Hohag
and Lori Jacobson

Published by

THE CHILD'S WORLD

Mankato, Minnesota

The Library —
A Magic Castle

Come to the magic castle
When you are growing tall.
Rows upon rows of Word Windows
Line every single wall.
They reach up high,
As high as the sky,
And you want to open them all.
For every time you open one,
A new adventure has begun.

Dan opened a Word Window. He read . . .

One fall day Squirrel saw this sign.

6

"I will bake my best acorn pie for the pie contest," she said.

And she did.

The pie was still hot when Mouse came by.
"My," said Mouse. "What a fine pie."

"Will you cut the pie in two pieces . . .

one half  for me,

one half  for you?"

"No," said Squirrel. "This pie is for
the pie contest. If I win, I will share
my pie with you."

Then Frog came by. "My," said Frog.
"What a fine pie."

"I do like acorn pie," he said. "Will
you cut the pie in three pieces . . .

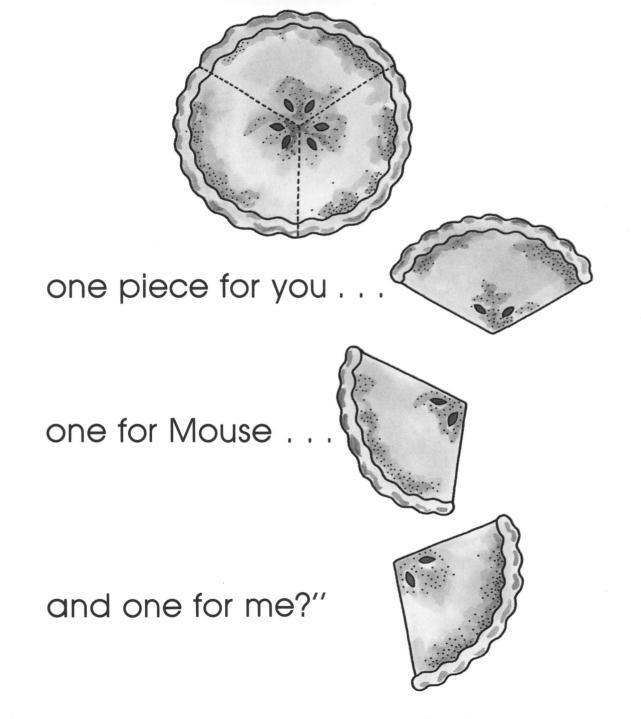

one piece for you . . .

one for Mouse . . .

and one for me?"

"No," said Squirrel. "This pie is for the pie contest. If I win, I will share my pie with you."

The pie was still hot, so Squirrel
put it in the window to cool.

Then the three friends went for
a walk in the woods.

While they were gone, Pig came by.
"My," said Pig. "What a fine pie."

"I will try just one little bite of pie.
Very good," she said.

Then Pig ate another bite. "It is just right," she said.

Pig ate and ate and ate until she cleaned the plate.

Just then Squirrel and her friends came by.
"My pie!" cried Squirrel. "Why did you
eat my pie?"

"Was your pie for my pie contest today?"
asked Pig. "It was," said Squirrel.

Pig took something out of her pocket. "Surprise! You win my pie contest," she said. "Your pie was the very best."

"That is not fair," said Mouse.

"Not fair at all," said Frog. "You ate the whole pie that we were going to share."

"I did not mean to eat the whole pie,"
said Pig. "I will try to make things right."

Pig ran outside and found more acorns.

"Squirrel makes the best pies of all," said
Pig. "Maybe she will make one more."

Squirrel did make one more pie. She cut it into four pieces, so everyone had a fair share.

Read some ways to cut Squirrel's pie.

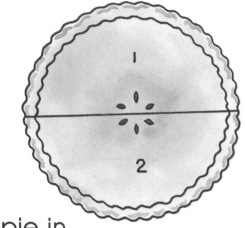

$\dfrac{1 \text{ pie in}}{2 \text{ pieces}}$

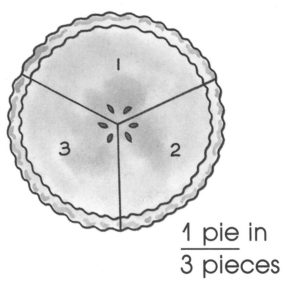

$\dfrac{1 \text{ pie in}}{3 \text{ pieces}}$

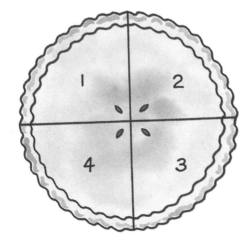

$\dfrac{1 \text{ pie in}}{4 \text{ pieces}}$